Praise for The World Exactly

The events of Sunnylyn's poems are quotidian transubstantiation. We are brought into a communion where the phenomena of the apparent becomes an apparition of what's been communicated to us. Musical and spiritual resonances arise as absence is invoked in the remains of what's left. The impersonal traumas of the body meet the personal traumas of the world. "What would it look like/if we left this place" sings the ghostly chorus.

— James Yeary

Sunnylyn Thibodeaux's poems hold an almost indescribable quality of intimacy, of nearness. In its freely melodic subtle though acute turns and shifts her ardent, lucky readers have come to cherish, *The World Exactly* carries a meditative, keenly perceptive, loose and wily music. Accompanied by an ever-expanding world vision, these vulnerable lyrics are freshly carved as today's mango as the world burns. Lest we go too far along her cosmic reach into infinity, she has us put on some folk music, or some Lou Rawls. We could put this book on a turntable. Faithful to the actual, inherently political, "we are in desperate search of a back-up planet"–Thibodeaux traverses global disaster, family, motherhood, illness, death, all while living on the brink in our urban, infested, corporatized scapes. If you can only buy one poetry book this year, buy this one, or sneak it in your pocket. *The World Exactly* arrives just as our trust in the actual is under so much scrutiny. Thibodeaux is brave enough to tell us why we must stay alive: "that we make it to know love in its boundless array of faith. That we make it to know love."

— Gillian Conoley

The World Exactly

The World Exactly

Sunnylyn Thibodeaux

CUNEIFORM PRESS

Variations of some of these poems have previously appeared in *Amerarcana, Apocalypse Art 2020, As Of Late, Banqueted, Can We Have Our Ball Back, Cape Cod Poetry Review, Cencer, Dispatches: Poetry Wars, Elderly, Entropy, High Noon, Paradise Now, Poetry Now, Positive Magnets, Queen Kong, SFMOMA's Open Space, A Sharp Piece of Awesome, So & So Magazine, spoKe, Trampoline,* and *Yes Poetry.* Some of these poems have also been included in the chapbooks *What's Going On* (Bird & Beckett) and *Witch Like Me* (The Operating System).

Copyright © 2020 Sunnylyn Thibodeaux
ISBN: 978-1-950055-08-1

Published by:
Cuneiform Press
www.cuneiformpress.com

Distributed by:
Small Press Distribution
1341 Seventh Street
Berkeley, CA 94710-1409
Tel. (800) 869-7553
www.spdbooks.org

CONTENTS

Confirm Humanity	13
Electric System	14
[Oh heavens]	15
What Better Time to Open Up the Zohar?	16
Memorial Day	17
Morning Survey	18
Neighborhood Outtakes	20
Fire Lake Haven	21
Bring Me Flowers	29
Bells Are Ringing Out/Big Fish Oddity	30
The Dark Center of the Universe	32
We Eat Cakes of Kings	33
It's in the Way You Fold Your Hands	35
[The young sage]	36
Such Great Heights	37
Future Weather or Beside the State Capitol	38
When You're Silent Long Enough You Can Hear the Afterlife	39
Rings of Herald	41
The Deal	42
[A silk covered Hunger Moon]	44
Oh! You Pretty Thing	45
Connectivity from the Outside In	46
The Truths Have All Been Converted	47
The Space Between Sound	49
March 23, 2017	50
A Well-Respected Man	51
Saint Joseph's Day	53

"It's not time for light"	54
The Ides of March is Overdue	55
Radio Sun Giant	56
Wasteland & Sanctimony	57
Coin-Operated	58
Desperate Measures	59
Nootropics in Composition	60
New Found Black Hole is Too Big for Theories to Handle	61
There's Static When You Drag Your Feet for Sound	63
Stars Tell Us Winter Has Come	64
Powell Street, December	65
Approximate Thought as it Goes Astray	66
Seasonal Affective Disorder	67
Mystery Tramp, Church & Market	68
Kish-a-Mish, revisited	69
It is February	70
Sound & Vision	71
Camp Fire in Paradise	72
May Day, a Decade or So Later	73
Hayward Faultline	74
Goldman Trophy	75
Outbound 9 AM	76
In the Vicinity	77
Apparitions	78
Lucky Charms	79
Today's Poem	80
What's Going On	81

For my father
whose perspective
allows both
flight & stance

I
Can-
not
accord
sympathy
to
those
who
do
not
recognize
The human crisis

—— Jack Spicer

CONFIRM HUMANITY

Soft greys break
in stratocumulus developments
nude light backing forms
Yesterday desperation took hold
of a man in a market
as he eliminated himself
on the aisle with Charmin near
What measures value
of existence beyond
judgements and conditioning
The House
will vote today
on conduct unbecoming
to the forty-fifth leader
and chief. Despite the storm
which has only dampened
miseries of the street
sky's illuminated
golden peach
with aptitude
and transformation

ELECTRIC SYSTEM

We've got King tides
and Alice Coltrane sweeping
up the mood. It's Christmas Eve
and Japantown is overrun with littered
umbrellas and nitro puffs. Safeway smeared
with footprints and a Salvation
Army Santa playing a recorder
with his little red collection bucket. An emergency
landing at SFO. Rain is still pouring
through a hole in the roof. 94-year-old
landlord stopped in yesterday to say hello. *Shit
came out when he saw the gape. Get an estimate*
Rent hasn't been cashed making the account
seem inflated for delight. Santa Tracker
is running despite the government's
shutdown over a lack of empathy and an orange
man's temper tantrum. The spirit of giving
doesn't live in everyone. It isn't supposed to
Our shoulders are strong, and we will
continue to carry joy into the night
across borders of religion and race
because that one wish is the persistent hope
that we make it to know love in its
boundless array of faith. That we make it
to know love

Oh heavens
        high above   how
    orchestrated
        are   your   hands
  for this l o n g
        n o t e   to carry
              til morn
How reflective
        the night
            sky
    when it's
        weighted
            with such of

      s t a r s

            the gods are angry still
            it'll be a slow moon
                to rise

WHAT BETTER TIME TO OPEN UP THE ZOHAR?

for David Meltzer

Lorca's in the tub singing
about the rescue of America
in some gospel sounding croak
I'm staring at the framed Berman
image for Luna's cover recalling how
it functioned as some sort of 12-step
program's guide during a bad run
How you chuckled with sincerity
and good tales of bad runs
of famed poets. Spinning
the light to assure I knew I was
in good company. I'd give a left
just to be Lamantia hiding from you
on the other side of the street
It would ensure that you're still here
and I could tell you of Lorca's songs
and how she views the world exactly
the way you would've taught her to

MEMORIAL DAY

All that's left is the shroud
                        the back wings. Roaches
scurrying in the kitchen. There's no
greater threat than this time at hand
     Drunken cackles from the street. Still damp
                        from 4 AM rain
I missed the instructions for this part. The trap
Deflate of dream. Utopia was always
supposed to be right at hand. Right and left
Any which way we'd make of it

                         Marine layer
won't budge for the rumble under our feet. Sky
tears open in the north. Sirens
on high. A small pool forms
in the buckle of asphalt
In its gentle tremble
the reflection of the grey
white mass overhead
with a perfect seam of blue
The rift where
the dead speak
how-tos

MORNING SURVEY

My slanted ear
picks up a telephone's ring
not digitally compromised
but old school
bell and hammer dings
I can never tell the direction
from which sound travels
The monster garbage
eating truck swallows
all pleasantries
the preschool windchime gone
the sparrows' tweets
the notes of Belle & Sebastian through the screen
At some point
threw a seed in a pot
It has since sprouted
but I cannot recall its genus
likely a lemon seed spit
from my water 3 years ago
It stands a foot tall
with its glossy green
leaves but can't really say
if bearing fruit is
in its future
A neighbor
put out a knife set
in its butcher block
orchestration along with

a box television and a sleeping bag
nearly making the street
inviting
How have we come to view
necessities as disposable?
How have we come to view
disposables as necessity?
The garbage monster ate
every thing in a series
of grumbles and crunches
and has moved
down the hill
Somewhere
in front or behind
left or right
a baby
is crying its heart out

NEIGHBORHOOD OUTTAKES
for R. Dillon

Mountain
out of a molehill is a sure sign she's done
Thank you for the tv and the jukebox poems
Mardi Gras bead pick-up and diamonds. Wet mud
clumps tripped up baby feet   dog's dazed
on frisbee glop.   There are dangling hearts
all across the intersections of NOPA. Yours
all knotted in NY. Good company
to work out influences. 28 lb
dog rushes my bum knee   across the way
                 a hippie giggles from his van
She was asleep before I even got home
and I haven't opened the book, haven't
washed my hands. Staring at the city
            workers breaking from chopping
            a perfectly healthy tree. I'm protesting
            this by writing you a poem   using
            up the last pages of my notebook
This isn't meant to be ironic
I hate ironic poems
       There was a hawk tangled in some line
       at the other end of the park. I'm waiting
       to hear of a rescue. It reminds me of you

FIRE LAKE HAVEN

with Kenneth Rexroth

The warm air flows imperceptibly seaward;
The autumn haze drifts in deep bands
Over the pale water;
White egrets stand in the blue marshes

i.
Smoke is waiting
to roll hills
sweep bridges
as they link the haves
      and have nots
grey pink orange and tan
like a wall holding
back an army

      Pressure on
to activate my core. Relearn
posture. Position myself
at a plywood covered window
across from where Rexroth
held court. Above a record store
that never has hours of operation
for a slow hunt in language
as it was first known. We often
forget song as works
           of enlightenment

Wall pushes slowly
wind changes angles

ii.
         On Mars
a heat probe mole
that was to dig 10-16 feet
underground was spat out
by the red orb. We are in
desperate search of a back-up
planet

iii.
Bagpipes
         in the distance
gadgets tinkering, wind-up toys
Mind Field, Kirchart love. I want
to crawl on the floor to figure it out
to figure my figure
         Bloody hang nail
         Tight hamstring
         Breathe. Hold

Wind has splintered branches
on Chinese Elms and Mulberry
         all Poplars felled
         windows rattle

iv.
         In the aftermath
         of gluttony
         there's indifference
         believing one's
         loss is another's gain
This is how monster lives form

(a *need* morphed from a want)

Little birds take flight
They understand well before we do

Sun skirts horizon without an arc
without a sound, dusty winds traversing
golden slivers slide down the wall—
    little geometries of light
      fluctuating energies
          tremble in the troposphere
            Hello, friend

v.
It is fire season
    all animals know
things we're too big
-headed to acknowledge
Plants wilt
in low hanging autumn sun
        dead leaves fall
          particulate in the air
            chokes us out

There's an atmospheric weight
There's an existential weight
    There are more books to read
        than I have space for

vi.
        Smoke is waltzing
in valleys, out to Farallon's

around the peninsula
while winds whip embers
golden berries jump
cross highways
Brush fire starts in Crockett

vii.
                Scientists have pinpointed
the homeland of modern humans
to Botswana. Shifts in climate
allowed fertile corridors to open
to migration. 130,000 years ago
It is presumed acid rain
killed the dinosaurs. The Sumatran elephant
has made it to the endangered species list
as well as the orangutan and the South
China tiger. We've consumed
and gathered trophies and treats
only to weep at misfortune
        crying out
           oceans full of plastic

              Here comes the wall
purple sandstone cloud, winds
smother us in our greed. Bears
hunt. Cougar watching flight

viii.
Deeply layered in mother earth
are our tongues, our sins, and our remedies
Beyond our attempts, we will repeat fate
Microbes and fungi will recolonize

        Call out woes and glories
        to heavens, vibrations
        that hold energies
        for a conjure of specters/ancestors

          My spirit
is the egret
bridging worlds. The positioning
of my spine needs support. Our
positioning needs work. Trees
slanting in the winds. Windows
shaking in wooden frames. Here
comes ash in its flurries
          dusting

ix.
          The Kincaid fire grows
to 74,000 acres. Another red flag warning
10 reps, left right bird dog
10 reps, heel slide

          Rexroth holds
the dearest translation of Reverdy
in my opinion. Slim
hard-to-find volume. No
big game hunter. Pure
romance and street
        Jazz ardor, "lyric absolute"
        Backbone figure

Same streets, Western
Addition watching smoke

shade the hills. Watching properties
flip for the millions. The quality
of air yellow, orange, red, swift
                Refresh. Refresh

x.

Marsh fire at Grizzly Island
charcoal smoke swamp factor
with 3 heron rookeries
and 9 species of raptor
Expected to be contained

xi.
                Green daylight
hours. The Cypress shed
limbs. Savoy blue full
of chatter
from the parrots
that roam
Mt Diablo at dusk
lavender and rose
watching stars form
Wide crescent smile
of la luna
out west, amber hue
The water bearer in the northeast
2 sets, 15 reps clamshell
"Speed of Life"
            Breathe

xii.
      It is All Hallow's Eve
our witches are brewing
with herbs for restoration
Kincaid doubles containment
children fueled
on variations
of sugar
and its substitutes
Darkness coming
earlier as we roll t'wards winter
after the warmest summer on record

xiii.
      The lift of All Saints Day's light
Fresh flowers for stained stones
Kincaid 68% contained
Our yellow fighters
are worn and heroic
pale hazed sunrise
Lumbar bridge, hold

      Earth's gravity arched
      the trajectory
      of an asteroid
      as it swept
      less than 4,000
      miles from southern Africa
The Mitochondrial Eve
is being disputed
questions of how Denisovans
and Neanderthals fit in. A bend

in the course
> "The place is on a mission
> Before the Night owl
> Before the animal noises"

xiv.
      Dia de los Muertos hovering
Orange yellow sensors
morning dew on a green soccer field
sugar skulls: pink, blue, marigold
Kincade, 72% contained
77,758 acres burned
372 structures destroyed
some evacuation lifted
    Things are looking up
     however much to grasp

> *Strong ankled, sun burned, almost naked,*
> *The daughters of California*
> *Educate reluctant humanists;*
> *Drive into their skulls with tennis balls*
> *The unhappy realization*
> *That nature is still stronger than man.*

                            Oct 25–Nov 2, 2019

BRING ME FLOWERS

                              Sun is glazed over
                              in a residue
                              of moisture and pollutants
The thyme is browning
on its edges
though the soil is still damp

            A plentiful weed has joined
                    this caged garden
       I hope it will
               bring me flowers

BELLS ARE RINGING OUT/BIG FISH ODDITY

It's nearing 7 AM, sky is muted
with its moisture blanket. Spent
last hour with Kaufman's outlook
from the inside
of our less humane streets
although most are going by the same
name. Now with Tarkovsky. My heart bends
a little in compassion for lands
and times I somehow know
Rodney Reed's stay
is all the joy of this morning's coffee
with its cinnamon grit and oily drops
Dense fog advisory
won't lift for a couple more
rounds of hands. A friend lost
one of her babies in the womb
with 4 more weeks to go
while the brother readies himself
for this broken world. Could I
offer anything of comfort
in this white out morning?
A notebook and pen for grief letters to come
An embrace for the experience of receiving emptiness
Solace in children's nature of knowing
when spirits enter a room
Open heavenward
more than arms
and say a word

for the Scorpios
All arranging
and orchestrating chords
orange lights with dust
far off in the distant
realm of things we only know
when we're silent long enough
I've got your hand
here. His too. Sun
behind marine's cloak
Steam of coffee, cinnamon tint
Grief shrouds all hours of the day
no matter its fragile light. Hope
as a forgotten burning behind the sky
with its layers and palls and musicality

THE DARK CENTER OF THE UNIVERSE
for Gerrit Lansing

Sickly spells wrestle deep
                round five, day 8
Death has a way of chipping at the heart
                little takes of light to pocket
    He should be golden by now
The cherry blossoms are lustrous
                and fragrant
Cassiopeia in her winged formation. Plastic babies
                stuffed in cakes

How can beauty fall so hollow in this month of renewal?
                Oh right—it took you too

WE EAT CAKES OF KINGS
for Shay Zeller

Wolf
moon
hangs
over
bend
of
river
Crickets
chirp
and
mosquitoes
swarm. We
snuck two
green papayas
from a neighbor
's tree and four
blood oranges
from another

Clouds
    stack stories
        of cumulus
      creatures
An elephant
    shifts to cover
the circle of luminance above
        and we
        stuff our stolen

                              fruit like secrets family
                                    keeps. The crook
                                         of river
                                              having shifted
                                                    long ago
                                                  depositing
                                                  remnants
                                              of what came
                                            here before we
                                          stumbled forth
         Little bands
                  march along
                          curves
                             forgetting
                             names
                          of all
                       the owners
                    of men

IT'S IN THE WAY YOU FOLD YOUR HANDS

Kentridge's *Refusal of Time*
surrounds circus like
in its charmed political rhythm
I want it as a backdrop
       to a daily routine—
              dark and playful
                    to structure and erase
                    restructure and efface
Crowds unsure
of their placement. I wanted
              to rotate
              chairs at every screen blink
                    change perspectives
              for the hands behind the head told an
overlapping
              story that had to do with breath, had to
              do with the way movement enters a room
Traditional beliefs have been developed
as adaptive survival strategies
              forever fated to operate
              seconds behind schedule
a delay resistant to control

```
The young sage
              leans left
              after brutal
              November winds
                              A haze
                           is lingering
                                    unable
                              to catch
                                    the drift
              Politics
           has found
       its way
              into
                    everything
```

SUCH GREAT HEIGHTS

Yesterday, we watched a rat weave
in and out of brambled branches
to steal what someone had left for the birds
An offering nonetheless

      Monsters with their crater faces sink
      in infantile thunder and luster
      Quick grab hands
           from ours to yours

      Something fell from the sky

It is the lies we tell our children
that will one day sing us low
Crumbling civilizations
rocks of purest red

"It is by the pull of abysses that you measure height"

      The birds all shake their heads disapprovingly

FUTURE WEATHER OR
BESIDE THE STATE CAPITOL

There's a history that is known
        and neglected for torment
            that can't be let go. There are song birds
                    that throw their voices and clouds
                    that send dragons down
In and out of a wood frame
wasps make their way
                buzzard circles high
There are so many past lives
that we've shaken hands with
and those we've stepped over
            (persons prescribed to you)
        that we've neglected the energies in this room
Everyone has an image they hold on to
                of themselves
                of you
It never matters how time changes us
        mannered. diseased. heightened
They hold on for an understanding
of themselves. Fear at its base
            for the clouds could take them
            and the birds could hold their tongues

WHEN YOU'RE SILENT LONG ENOUGH YOU CAN HEAR THE AFTERLIFE
for Diane di Prima

Outside
horns
interrupt
melody
    (if one
    could hear
    a tune)
        How
            rain
        gives
            sound
        How
            wind
        rings
            chime
The Mexican
sage with
its velvety
brush
quivers
    And someone
    got stuck
    on Nationalism

Our voice
    under heel
Our pen
    tucked

    deep
into
damp
soil
so the dead
  can
    scribble
   tiny
  notes
in
  the
    night
      giving
        us
         indication
       of
     how
    to
   turn
around

RINGS OF HERALD

Today is Mardi Gras back home
      everyone's taken to the streets

Here, in
chilling blue
little buds
are bursting
      forth
and our eyes
keep shifting
to an unnatural
      state of things
in various news. Will
      this be
our unifier? Will
      this be
our demise?
    The earth
     gives us
      many things
and some
in strange
disguises. Never
overlook
the power
of a nuisance
weed. Dandelions
have medicine
in many forms

THE DEAL

The sunflowers have come
to bloom as we lay
our little bird down
There are sirens
on all edges
of this square—
anniversary of the quake
Chest quivers empty

Started these pots
seven years back
in a grieving process
for my unborn. Some
didn't pull through
bad air days. Some
stunted in growth. Some
shocked with a transfer

I wanted to save the bees
and ourselves
so went with flowerings
and herbs. Then someone
gave me a young lemon
tree treated with neonicotinoid
I felt relief
when it was stolen

My daughter wants another pet
I say, "give it time"
meaning, give *me* time
and re-water the shriveling
flower bed checking
for aphids and hungry caterpillars

A silk covered Hunger Moon
rises large and round
over a damp soccer field
where mosquitoes swarm
in strange November
humidity

        My daughter's last
        scrimmage of the season
        while I swat blood
        suckers from my neck

    It's over

"I am thirsty," she says
    "What's for dinner?"

OH! YOU PRETTY THING

We've broken our spell
with hollyhock and chrysanthemum
having navigated darkness
just some months ago
                Speedy ants are carrying
                mountains to their queen
When we are serving so devotedly
why do we take the abuse of men?
As if we've forgotten to do for ourselves
Navigation sits on tips
          of tongues if we allow
          silence to let it form
300 ants work the crevice
under a Meyer lemon tree
bring morsels to the reproductive
element of their colony. Her needs
are met. The work mothers do
is witchcraft to some

CONNECTIVITY FROM THE OUTSIDE IN
for Jason Morris

Everything points to Desert Music. Dry brittle wind
Dry brittle posture. Siren at the mark of half day. Sun
doesn't peek for the trees. Fragmented light carried
in the ash of stirring
      In Iceland lava is spewing
from the cracks. The flanks of Bardarbunga
eyed with pressure, mystery. A moderate tempo. Heat
from within came without. Steam. Sulphur dioxide
Orchestrate
    The Creator Has a Master Plan
Known to cause respiratory problems. Dry brittle
wind. Magma pushing forth. We are part of it
Transcendence. Dainty feet. The mundane life
It has nothing to do with a rib. The flanks
The fissures. Summer something mountain top. Sub-
surface stream. There are white flowers on the water
Lava flowers on the water. Geologically
speaking, it could go any which way
        Time tells
tales. They were said to be the first but Isha
was doomed from the get-go. The very best gift
comes from the heart

THE TRUTHS HAVE ALL BEEN CONVERTED
for Lorca Ballard

A book was given from above
is how the story goes, one of the versions
of mans' knowledge. We come
from the earth in a way that is
different than their kind. Our knowing
spreads from a center
where nerve endings
cross in complexities—solar at least
Enoch as dismissed was likely not
a mother's decision. Raziel, keeper
of mysteries, may appear to reveal
things beyond our original scope
        The willow bends to form embrace
        The dandelion floats wishes to cracks & crevices
        medicines for many ails
        There are things to know
        as modes of survival
                (An army comes to land
                      trumpets blast in afternoon sun
                              quick! retrieval)
There is an entrance and an exit
to every occasion, beginning and end
There are no hooves here, but fire
as mystery, magic and life
The things to know were always right here
Don't let them teach you beauty
as anything different
as anything the same

Be as quick as you may be slow. There is all the time
There is no time. In you
is everything already

THE SPACE BETWEEN SOUND

                    I've got riddles to tell
That North Star in the east is actually Venus
before dawn. There's a trajectory
the father and messenger will follow
                    Over seas women've known
a call unlike the others. We are water
in our pull. We are hidden oranges
and sprigs bounded by carnelian
Venus rising from spilled seed

This here red ribbon on the bed
shapes itself like a staff. It came
with a gift of chocolate from a mother
Some nights little sleep rests
Some hours stars twinkle in appearance
through atmospheric dust smearing edges
we cannot see. White blue streaks. In out flex

An orchestration beyond measure
and complications we've piled upon
by our own ignorance. Debris in light and
sound. Fragments. Some cross over

It is omens that all come down to alignment

MARCH 23, 2017
for Joanne Kyger

How do you right a poem
when the sky is bursting forth
with radiant blue and
clouds are formed
with that of a sculptor's hand
and somehow you, in your absence
from this earth, are everywhere
sparrow bobs
wind chime tones
palms bend
and the news hammers
home that things are way
out of control

    [come back]

A WELL-RESPECTED MAN
for Kevin Killian

With time handed over
    sun and clear blue morn
        clank of metal and cement
            as workers break down scaffolding
                with street and safety talk. Spanish
            words I only recognize fragments
        of while waiting for a digital
tune to alert that the cycle is complete

Don't spend too much time with lines of the hand
                          stories aren't told that way

      There is time
              and fresh ribbon
                for the Royal
                that leaves holes
                in place of Os

Franz Schubert's the Trout tones as an anthem set for a bugle
in its digital calling. Whites are ready to be hung

                Sunflower seeds
    planted last Monday
    have busted their black shells
                green sprouts

            My neighbor
is coughing, never opens his window

>   for the chill. He can be heard
>   through walls. Smell his habits
>   seeping in

My mind drifts to Kevin
>   how I wanted to talk about the shadows
>   in Spain. The histories. Streets
>   how I wanted to talk. More. Again

>   The lace curtains
>   need a wash after traffic
>   has sent its dust for a dozen years

Some things collect like that
when given proper placement

A Lou Rawls record and another cup of black coffee
should clean the slate enough for remembrance
>   A hand carved pipe. Frankincense
>   Tobacco Road shifted light

Farewell Transmission now opens

>   *The whole place is dark*

>   and he is here. And not
>   at the same time

SAINT JOSEPH'S DAY

I caught Frida Kahlo
over my shoulder
as I waited for results
at the doctor's office
Unsure what to make of
her company I treated myself
to a lesson in Japanese whisky
and pronunciation of Turkish
wines. My problems are likely
tethering. My problems likely
have histories. The rest of the
feelings were held in the curl
of my toes. Where else
were they to go. I spent a lot
of money in the shops. Thinking
about Frida and Reverdy and
Valrhona chocolate, a veil of health
as death rows on someone's shore

We all dress ourselves one last time

"IT'S NOT TIME FOR LIGHT"

Dark grey flame stretching south
broken striations for song
The chill is damp between walls
                silence, mojo rising
We will wake to bomb threats, a negative balance
little bird with his chest thrusts and bobs
City inspector will be out again to survey the habitability
of our habitat. One garbage can and two pots catch rain
                plaster specks, mossy growths
Lost angels on the streets
begging for acknowledgement
their eyes hazily reflecting neighbor's
Christmas lights. We will nod
in passing. I've got nothing to give
but the knowledge that they are there. Winter
will burn us into early deaths. Our lung, your mind-game,
his needle. The good that has come
through this place is stitched heavily into fabrics
and stories. Stitched deep beyond thread. There was
good before someone dropped
the albatross from sky. Fellows
got places they aren't even
sure exist. As waters rush round
we got notions
and a shelter of street

THE IDES OF MARCH IS OVERDUE

Every day we are faced with beauty and corruption
and words we forget the meaning of and boundaries
we're not comfortable with. Down on the street
there's litter rustling in patterns that no one gives
thought to. Down in the canyon rents raise
I can't help checking calendars for the next full
moon, for the next stone fruit season. Tomorrow is
my favorite wine drinking friend's birthday. She's in
New York and we don't talk news of war anymore
Take it all for granted. Litter is worse. Preoccupation
with cures. I wonder about cities and who makes
them news. And when stone fruit will return
and when the moon will find its way
back into conversation
no matter how
many miles
to go

RADIO SUN GIANT

In a shift of high noon, we went
over hills with ankle roll debris
tangled ivy, rotted branches broken
from some storm, everyday
plastics for consumerists, and needles
marking a time before Godric fell
SF has lost its signal
Lonely city, empty shell
of wealth in disposables
There are echoes of good faith
Someone holds its moment in a poem
shivers. A sperm whale is dead
with its belly full of single use

WASTELAND & SANCTIMONY

Somehow Benny Spellman
        always comes on my soundtrack
        or Dodo Bird iteration. It is blasted
grey out in May
when the colorful culture collide
of Carnaval is in full swing in the Mission

There have been 48 more shootings since Easter Sunday
                It's starting to lose
                its effect. People are dying
                nonetheless. No one
is talking about leopard sharks or grey whales
or that the Morganza has been opened again in less than 10 years
There are deniers
There are theorists
There are green dollars to be made
Some of us are so overwhelmed
with cross-stitches of surviving
        we've forgotten
        how to make conversation
Things seem too much. This fog won't burn
The abuse some of us find natural
has never had any harmony

COIN-OPERATED

There's loneliness
in the crowded laundromat
and a desperation
illuminated by surging
fluorescent lights. Pressing
into the wall I bury
my nose in Lansing's ode
to Jonas. My heart
aches for good company—
quick disputes
over others' verse or rise
to fame. How we miss
our friends and every
less obvious opportunity
but never more
than how much we miss
ourselves

DESPERATE MEASURES

A 4-watt flickered out
while the upstairs neighbor
with a hollow laugh
did his usual 1 AM routine
I want to blare Louie
Prima's *Oh Marie*
but we're sandwiched with
an elder that has already
paid for his sins by the way
he holds his wrists
Cracks in plaster
run for tales a century back
One of us will die
before the other two
One of us is having a harder go

NOOTROPICS IN COMPOSITION

A rusty hue before sun broke
the horizon. Jupiter and Antares in play
at the south's end, a translucent moon
floating out west. Survived
another night in this body, mind
racing with its ticker tape
hands trembling with light
Mercury—the mode of flatterers
in retrograde so things turn out
as they turn

NEW FOUND BLACK HOLE IS TOO BIG FOR THEORIES TO HANDLE

      Static builds
      in the mind
      and soot
      collects
      on chandeliers

We haven't got the means
to go it alone
or to fetch an arriving train
Anthems come. Little
did we know
    the high horse carries troubadours
    and people with small minds
Is this war that we are experiencing?

The fastest moving particles cannot escape
at 40 billion times the mass of the sun

    Someone is winning a misstep
      or counting beats with their tongue
      or receiving a label without compromise

When we get closer to the hole
we can see its bottomlessness
    black wind circles
        familiar eyes that form

Here's looking at you, kid

A zone of incineration
as darkness flatters
and overlords
crawling
on floors
seem to know our names
          Come on down

Little avalanche upon us
footfalls in a dust. Devils'
licks on a cloud

THERE'S STATIC WHEN YOU DRAG YOUR FEET FOR SOUND
for Anselm Berrigan

If not for the draft
from old windows

sitting askew in their frame
you could think it's summer

Dull hours of floor games
and Fantasmagory reading

I cringe at NPR's interview
about power and greatness

Crunching loud on seeded
crackers and black

garlic so that my head
sounds out something

different than the reality
that keeps catching

like dust in ice
cold beams of sun

STARS TELL US WINTER HAS COME

The child has a deep cough
which keeps our ears
tuned. Little sleep
for wicked spell
Mercury has changed
his rotation again
And we are up all
night deciphering
codes of tidal dissipation
We gravitate to each
corner for comfort, to
each other for observation
All wires in this house
hum and there's not a
single fraction of light
to tell us which words
to collect for use
        Heavy weight is felt
        Disturbance a rarity
        At six o'clock we shift green, then grey
        and the frame stands firm and hollow

POWELL STREET, DECEMBER

These streets have a muted glisten
with its litter now stuck in the damp
A femme with extravagant lashes
stands cock-hipped in a wig cap
while she holds her locks
in one hand, she stuffs dollars
with her other into a peach satin bra
A bum at the corner
straddles a milkcrate
with a sogged sign
that reads, "Spread
the cheer. Spare change"
A millennial holds
up her cross-eyed company
as she eats a packaged danish
with its yellowed dough
Shoppers bust through
crowds with bags
that are no longer
free with purchase
A trolley grinds past
operator dinging a thudded Jingle Bells
Tourists beaming
at an open view
of a city that's lost
its love

APPROXIMATE THOUGHT
AS IT GOES ASTRAY

after John Wieners

Silver streaks of light
against a hazy blue

Raw gas in the wind
Workers with grand-maw beads
under hard hats in September sun

There is no thing such as silence
white noise shiftings

muted fade outs
of man's progression

All across the skyline
are shimmers of this lie
pounding asphalt
Birds take flight

A jet leaves a trail

We all have some other place
we must learn to be

SEASONAL AFFECTIVE DISORDER

Sky is a winter's blue
against a reluctant maple
still holding a dozen brown leaves
Stratus grey platforms out west
carry no threat of rain, but
a new river will be sent
in coming days. Pigeons
flap black in the shadows
of Kabuki. Busses
delayed for a monetary
check against a rich city's budget
Dysfunctional transit
in this slanted universe

MYSTERY TRAMP, CHURCH & MARKET

Motörhead was desired
but debate arose around cookies
and ethnic cuisine
Rain came on hard just
before morning snack
Clouds now fluff
in childhood patterns
while waiting for a bus
across from the bookstore
and bakery, a convert-
ible passes with a sappy
version of Elvis' "I can't help
falling in love with you"

KISH-A-MISH, REVISITED
(crabwalk under the stars)

for Logan Kroeber

Shadows of the three of us
cast on the mountain
from a porchlight set back
while stars unfolded, strewn
clusters luminous as a dusting on velvet
How our code of ethics finds a place in various sellabilities
How rational thought contradicts the gut
How the gut is corralled back round to such
                            sole purpose
We aren't alone in this wood
One darts across
a northerly spill
        fiery down

When there's nothing to see but burning out patterns
we get honest about the other

IT IS FEBRUARY
           for Duncan McNaughton

For your birthday
I'm thinking of Point Reyes Toma
and Lustau's Rare Cream Sherry
but am unsure if these would please you
in the state you're in. Older
our bodies seem to have a mind
of their own, while "experts"
scratch at what is left of theirs
The cherry blossoms are budding
I could lie that I orchestrated it
for your day, but as it has happened
in this city of avarice for longer than
my time it would be obvious as
untruth. And that may ruin our rapport
which will never do. So, I've scribbled
a note. To remind you that despite
the days untouched I am here
and you are always in my heart

SOUND & VISION

Sun rising coral sky
forty-seven degrees to shift
on right corner. Sealed up
for an escort. Pigeons flap
a shadow on the moss colored
wall. Across Bent and Omega

Final rise of the big star
for this Roman annual
Dust ourselves for tomorrow

We will burn curses as skies
lose luster again. Sink gold
shift rose, smoke,
lavender ilk

Friendships were lost
over diagnoses and gained
through witchcraft. Little
heart beats arrhythmically
We've got skullcap and parsnips
passionflower, lion's mane, and
black eyed peas for the troops
Peasantry has always served
our kind for purposes
of blending in
Polarized snapshots
Wicked tongue hold

That which rises in a wind

CAMP FIRE IN PARADISE

A fire-red sun over the cross tower
reflected in Pollard's "Waiting"
Pigeons aren't casting shadows
when we can hardly breathe
The gods, angry, turn their backs
Common energies have become unbalanced
indulgences that darken sight

Swells of consumption collapse
hidden truths of compassion

MAY DAY, A DECADE OR SO LATER

The bar is still there but the required balance has shifted
Hype has gone from swine flu to measles
and mass shootings, Trump's taxes, migrants
Not to mention some end of days is upon us

A cougar cub is dead in the Santa Monica mountains
from variants of strychnine. Environmental working group
has just released that California's drinking water
is contaminated with such toxins that 15,000 cases
of cancer could be blamed on it. And we were trying to stay hydrated
We were grieving for Flint

The truth we were once debating is still tangled possibly
worse than it was. There are variants of that too
            depending on which poet you're pocketing
              which gospel you're lifting. It's more Lou Rawls
now than Merle but we've got to ask my mama about Roland
doing a stint behind bars for drugs that Mac was carrying
                            The stories are richer
                                  if anything
I can't say the same for the replacements

HAYWARD FAULTLINE

Today's deluge has brought upon us
      the brim past the brink
Even the hills have divots for holding
Advisories keep bannering feeds
      red ribbon runs through
Tunneling earthworms rush to footpaths
      writhing through danger overhead
Burned out lands lacking root for hold
      shift with weight and gravity

Dormant seeds rejoicing
Domestics still grieving

Land shifted at 4:42 AM
For answers we are still
      looking t'wards the sky

GOLDMAN TROPHY

Micah, I told you
I'd write you a poem
while you shopped
for all particulars
that I've listed. I play
hard ball on how to
provide for the family
but it is really you
who gets it all
done. Give yourself
a pat or a one up
or a combo of sorts
Sometimes the hand
glides sloppily to keep
pace with the head
and you are out there
counting blocks, timing
your solo with puffs

OUTBOUND 9 AM

Train's ventilation system
has a noisy rhythmic hum
and two Chinese elders
talk across the aisle
in what settles as white
noise. Tunnel is still
as the delay lingers on
On the other end may
be daylight. May be
someone's trouble within
There can be little disturbance
in things we don't understand
The things we know
know us first

IN THE VICINITY

Bus crowded in rain
squeals its tires with a slip
on a train's track
trying for oomph
to take it uphill
Seniors and less
fortunate city dwellers
with their walking sticks
and busted out toes,
smell of urine, snuffed
cigarettes and mothballs, push in
for seats near the door. Everyone's
eyes appear closed, lids pulled
down in rest
or shame
or contemplation
about the forecast
Six days
at the bottom
of the ocean

APPARITIONS

With eyes closed
a Chinese Dragon
can be seen
white with a red mouth
golden trim ears
Keith Jarrett in Cologne
(there's a silhouette of a dark curly haired female)
I wonder how long we will last
in this falling down gentrifying space
Cancer. M.S. Deafness. Someone
is trying to kill me one way or another
but crumbling isn't anything
to be accustomed to

The dragon dances
its happy face in curves
right then left
Jarrett plays standing

LUCKY CHARMS

It is midafternoon. You are adrift
My head flutters with smiles of the dead
My heart aches. Rain let up
for a brief spell of warmth. More
to come tomorrow. Atmospheric river
sweeps in before we send it south, where
people are drowning sorrows in drink. Drunk
as a way of living. It could be mid afternoon
when the sky shifts to slate, a banjo rips
A neighbor is dead. His smile keeps me
company in the process of grief. We prepare
for rain with buckets to catch the drops
from a grand hole up above. In the cloud
formations I can see his teeth and legs
He was all teeth and legs. It is midafternoon
There is a banjo. And a hole

TODAY'S POEM

The parakeet sings and chuckles from his cage
which needs a good cleaning. MRI results
were emailed before bed on a day the doctor
is not in. I feel I'm intelligent enough
to decipher good news in the mix. But I am
no scientist
                   My neighbor has let me know
she cannot make the building meeting
I scheduled to discuss our hopes of staying
housed as our landlord gears up for 95 and has
slowed in cashing our checks. Sometimes 3 months
at a time. One must be strategic in consumeristic
tendencies. Her grandfather traveled yonder
way out in Connecticut and she'll return when
all settles. Things may fall down before they settle
I want to tell her, but I offer assistance however I can
Blanket gestures are often overlooked. But worse is
blanket oversight—when people are too self-consumed
to acknowledge your struggle. They struggle with recon-
ciliation of their own needs vs the world
                                       The app
on the phone tells me rain will hold off for several more
days, but clouds will stick around. I want quiet time
to reflect on my health. Or to take hold of my health. Or
to quit thinking about complications of this life and the
number of days left to us. What would it look like
if we left this place. If I stayed high all the time
How would I change my perspective if the doctor
called with bad news again. How tired can one be
and still give it everything

WHAT'S GOING ON

Because   out the window
                are distant things
right at hand   evergreen
      echoing   shift,   trimmed
            refinement of the new
      lofty neighbors   on the floor
I sit.   Close one eye to   storm cloud
                   We need rain

        The man with the machete is dead
     The world's greatest maternal figure
The tie
               Storm cloud doubles
On 4th Ave,   a mummified body   is removed
       from a foreclosed home.   To love those so
           To love those
                    To love

      Desperation   grows
      as   plants   wither. How the blood
clots will be watched.   Close both eyes.   Imagine
          the difference   No war of classes
        No war of cell against cell
                    No war

     Sky   blanketed   grey   white
Students missing
Musician slain   A shadowy   arrival

```
                        of the Great Pyramids at sunset
        Down low       never loses           esteem
                            in this view


                            The humble life
                    of trees.     They do not      beg
                    though they need.    They do not
                    grandstand and thieve.      Give
                                us shelter. Breath


        One hand.   Two      knife.   Twist
Our movements are tiny.            And
                        monstrous.   Our
                        movements    are mirrored
This goes       without saying.  The wound
from our hips stretches across time.  Close one eye
and its off in its own formation,    deciphering
        sides of a    new war.   Close both eyes
                            and they grieve


Because         out the window     everything
        else is stirring    clouds not holding      steady
shape,      gossip and pollen        flutter.   Rain clouds
                            prove         fickle
Maybe we weren't clear
in our expectations.        Maybe we didn't
communicate                 from the tree's stance


We need rain
We need—
        grace, sleep, food, peace
The shadows     that    are everyone
```

                else's story   shift   with the angle
            of the sun.   Shift   to this post
    and   that   forum.   Needs
                        so far buried,   begging
                            becomes the   unspoken
                                            Righteousness
                                                m u s h r o o m s
                                            despite the desert
                    Unnatural nature
                        of the world   at hand
    Out the window
                        revelations of the intelligent selves
                                drifting
                                        in   the   wind

We speak forgotten prayers
We thumb the beads
We genuflect
and kiss the feet

                        Something takes each and every one of us
                            no   matter   which   day   it   is

                        How we go
                                    depends   on   the heart

85

photograph by Lorca Ballard

Sunnylyn Thibodeaux was raised by a school bus driver and a taxi driver in a Sicilian Catholic home on a cul-de-sac sandwiched between the railroad tracks and the Mississippi River. Although she had a parish priest and a family psychic, she still felt blasphemed and from another lifetime. She took to writing in notebooks provided by her mother when her overall unease with the world proved to be engulfing. With confessions on the regular and Saint Joseph altars annually in her house, penance was a threaded part of her upbringing and held its weight in worldview, leaving the perceived only options for adulthood to either join the Peace Corps or become a teacher. So, she took the path that led the closest she could get to both—AmeriCorps. While studying education in New Orleans, she wrote a work of fiction about a grief-stricken man who wandered the snow with the hopes of getting to the moon, which caused a reaction in her professor that led her to switch gears to writing, but still ended up teaching in the South. Through good fortune, she landed in San Francisco for graduate school at New College of California where she fell into brilliant like-minded company. She spent years in the restaurant industry in various roles. The demand of which was a never-ending problem to solve. Recognizing the insanity, she opted for more domesticity. After becoming a mother, she joined a neighborhood association where she organized a playgroup for three years, raised funds for neighbors that experienced evictions due to fire, and instigated a movie night in the local park. She stays involved to argue against the pretentiousness of the changing neighborhood, and to ensure tenants are being protected. She began teaching again in the magical world of preschool. After Hurricane Katrina, she dreamed of going home to run a café that provided writing services for youth while functioning as an event space in the evenings, but she's afraid of behemoth flying insects. She goes back to New Orleans to renew her driver's license, and of course, for the seasons of King Cake and Sno-Ball. She always carries a notebook.

ACKNOWLEDGMENTS

Poems come as they come, but that is never without various influences through relations to and with the forces of the world. It would be inauthentic to not recognize the countless connections that light the path. I hold all the energies in esteem with abundant respect and amity. Thank you to Lorca for lighting everything anew and to Micah for keeping it all solid. I am forever grateful to Duncan McNaughton, Joanne Kyger, and David Meltzer whose company and verse is forever my compass. The support of many other luminaries tuning the ear, on the page and in the flesh is recognized. I owe you each an exchange of love: Will Skinker, Christina Fisher, Ryan Newton and Jackie Motzer, Neeli Cherkovski, Joseph Torra, Will Yackulic, Norma Cole, Catherine Curtin, Jason Morris and Sally Hahn, Derek Fenner, Nick Whittington, Jeff Butler, Michael Slosek, James Yeary, Sara Larsen, Garrett Caples, Rod Roland, Patrick Dunagan and Ava Koohbor, Colter Jacobsen, Sarah Cain, and of course my mom for the music, the wit and the notebooks. A special thanks to the editors of all the publications where many of these works appeared in some fashion.